CAUTION, READER!

The jokes in this book are extremely funny, silly, and at times **outrageous**. This may result in **snickering**, **snorting**, and **giggling** uncontrollably. You might laugh **so hard** your stomach hurts. You might laugh **so hard** you start to cry. It's entirely possibly you'll laugh **SO HARD** you fall off your chair. We do not recommend reading this book during quiet time or when your younger brother or sister is taking a nap. **Please read responsibly.**

Puffin Books by ROALD DAHL

ROALD DAHL

WHOPPSY-WHIFFLING

JOKE BOOK

Illustrated by **Quentin Blake**

PUFFIN BOOKS

PUFFIN BOOKS
An imprint of Penguin Random House LLC
375 Hudson Street
New York, New York 10014

First published by Puffin Books UK, 2016
Published by Puffin Books, an imprint of Penguin Random House LLC, 2018

Text copyright © 2016 by Roald Dahl Nominee Ltd, with contributions by
Ruth Reyes and Caitlin Baker
Illustrations copyright © 2016 by Quentin Blake

Puffin Books ISBN 9780451479303

Printed in the United States of America

1 3 5 7 9 10 8 6 4 2

WHOPPSY-WHIFFLING

JOKE

BOOK

Miss Trunchbull's BANNED school jokes

Tell these to your **friends** and you'll be thrown straight in the **chokey!**

Why did the teacher turn the lights on?
Because the class was so dim!

Who invented fractions?
Henry the Eighth!

Why was Miss Trunchbull worried?
Because there were too many rulers in school!

MISS TRUNCHBULL: What do we call the outer part of a tree?
BRUCE BOGTROTTER: **Don't know, Miss!**
MISS TRUNCHBULL: Bark, silly! Bark!
BRUCE BOGTROTTER: **Woof, woof!**

Why is six afraid of seven? **Because seven eight nine!**

"If you get on the wrong side of Miss Trunchbull, she can liquidize you like a carrot in a BLENDER."

TEACHER: Make up a sentence using the word "lettuce." PUPILS: **Let us out of school early!**

TEACHER: What are you reading?
PUPIL: **I dunno!**
TEACHER: But you're reading aloud!
PUPIL: **Yeah, but I'm not listening!**

If two's company and three's a crowd, what are four and five? **Nine!**

How did you find school today? **Well, I just got off the bus and there it was!**

TEACHER: You aren't paying attention. Are you having trouble hearing? PUPIL: **No, sir. I'm having trouble listening!**

How do bees get to school? **By school buzz!**

What is a snake's favorite subject? **Hiss-tory!**

What is an archaeologist?
Someone whose career is in ruins!

Why did the nose hate school?
It was tired of being picked on!

What happens when you take the school bus home?
The police make you bring it back!

What do elves learn in school?
The elf-abet!

What's the best way to get straight As?
Use a ruler!

What grade did the pirate get at school?
High Cs!

Which animal cheats in school?
A cheetah!

What's a witch's favorite subject?
Spell-ing!

What is a pirate's favorite subject?
Arrrrrt!

LITTLE BOY: I can't go to school today, I have a tummy ache.
MOM: **Where does it hurt?**
LITTLE BOY: In school!

How do you make the number one disappear? **Add the letter "g" and it's "gone"!**

Why did the teacher write on the window? **To make her lesson very clear!**

Why was the broom late for school? **He over-swept!**

Why didn't the skeleton go to the school dance? **He had no body to take!**

Bruce Bogtrotter's
BELLY LAUGHS

Are you ready for some **tasty** one-liners?

What's that fly doing in my gravy?
Looks like breaststroke!

What tables don't you have to learn?
Dinner tables!

What kind of nuts always seem to have a cold?
Cashews!

What is a pretzel's favorite dance?
The twist!

What are twins' favorite fruit?
Pears!

CUSTOMER: Waiter, this food tastes funny.
WAITER: **Then why aren't you laughing?**

Suddenly the boy let out a **gigantic BELCH** which rolled around the Assembly Hall like thunder. Many of the audience began to GIGGLE. "Silence!" shouted the Trunchbull.

What do computer operators eat for lunch?
Chips!

What would happen if pigs could fly?
The price of bacon would go up.

Waiter, will my pizza be long? **No, sir, it will be round!**

What happens if you make a walnut laugh? **It cracks up!**

Why did the banana go to the doctor? **Because it wasn't peeling well!**

What do you call a peanut in a spacesuit? **An astro-nut!**

What is green and sings? **Elvis Parsley!**

What cheese is made backward?
Edam.

What did the nacho say to the burrito?
Can we taco 'bout it?

Why did the baker stop making doughnuts?
She was bored of the hole business!

What type of cheese doesn't belong to you?
Nacho cheese!

Knock knock!
Who's there?
Justin.
Justin who?
Justin time for lunch!

CUSTOMER: Is there spaghetti on the menu today?
WAITER: **No, I cleaned it off!**

What did the Italian chef give his waiters?
A pizza his mind!

What do polar bears have for dinner?
Iceberg-ers!

Why couldn't the teddy bear eat his lunch?
Because he was stuffed!

Why did the tomato blush?
Because it saw the salad dressing!

What did the daddy tomato say to the baby tomato?
Hurry and ketchup!

What's worse than finding a worm in your apple?
Finding half a worm in your apple!

What's orange and sounds like a parrot?
A carrot!

How do eggs leave in an emergency?
Through the fire eggs-it!

What do aliens eat off in space?
Flying saucers!

What vegetable should never be served on a boat?
Leeks!

The **Roly-Poly Bird's**
JOKEY-WOKEYS

They'll make
you **squawk!**

What is the
strongest bird?
A crane!

Why does a flamingo
lift one leg?
**Because if it
lifted both legs it
would fall over!**

Why do birds fly
south for the winter?
**Because it's too
far to walk!**

What is black,
white, and red
all over?
**A sunburnt
penguin!**

What do you
call a seagull flying
over land?
A land-gull!

What do doctors give sick birds?
Tweetment!

Did you hear the joke about the broken egg?
It'll crack you up!

What's more clever than a talking bird?
A spelling bee!

What birds can you find in Portugal?
Portu-geese!

What is black and white, and black and white, and black and white, and black and white, and black and white?
A penguin rolling down a hill!

"**Please** don't mention **Bird Pie** again," said the Roly-Poly Bird. "It gives **me** the **SHUDDERS**."

Why do penguins carry fish in their beaks? **They don't have any pockets!**

SON: Mom, can I have a canary for Christmas?
MOM: **No, we'll have turkey like we always do!**

What do you call a sick bird of prey? **Ill-eagle!**

What do birds watch on TV? **Duck-umentaries!**

Where do tough chickens come from? **Hard-boiled eggs!**

14

What do you call a
bird in the winter?
Brrrrrrr-d!

What happened
when the turkey got
in a fight?
**He got the
stuffing knocked
out of him!**

What do
ducks have with
cheese?
Quackers!

Where would you find
a turkey with no legs?
**Precisely where
you left him!**

What's the most musical
part of a chicken?
The drumstick!

George's
MARVELOUS
MUM JOKES

(AND **DAD** JOKES! AND **LITTLE BROTHER** JOKES! AND **GRANDMA** JOKES!)

Fun for **all** the family!

What's it called when you have your grandmother on speed dial?
Insta-gran!

What does "maximum" mean?
A very big mother!

What does "minimum" mean?
A very small mother!

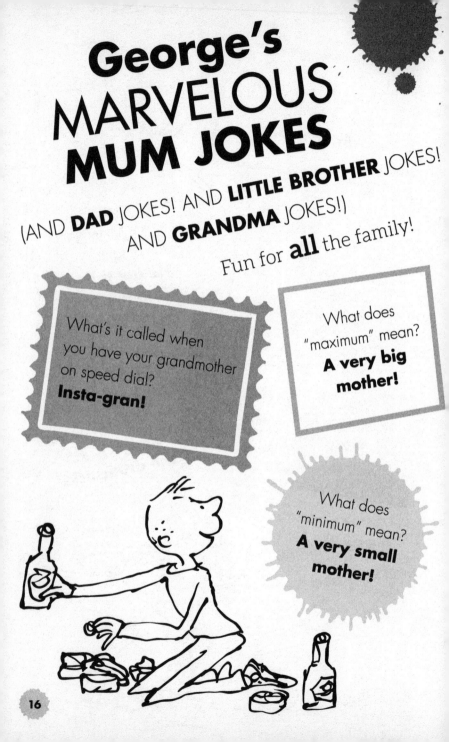

DAD: Why are you sitting on the cat?
DAUGHTER: **The teacher told us to write an essay on our favorite animal!**

What did the baby corn call its father? **Pop-corn!**

What did the digital watch say to the grandfather clock? **"Look, no hands!"**

Why was Dad running around and around his bed? **He wanted to catch up on his sleep!**

What bug
is related to you?
Your aunt!

FIREMAN:
Who knows what a
smoke detector is for?
LITTLE BOY:
**To tell Mom when
dinner is ready!**

What BIG
bug is related
to you?
**Your great
aunt!**

GEORGE: Mom, why is some of your hair gray?
MOM: **Every time you do something that
annoys me or Dad, one of our hairs turns
gray!**
GEORGE: So...why is *all* of Grandma's hair gray?

FRED:
My grammar's terrible!
GEORGE:
What's wrong with her?

My gran used to run an origami business, but sadly **it folded!**

Did you hear about the man who can jump from tree to tree?
He's a monkey's uncle!

Why doesn't Amy like her mom's brother?
He's a bit uncool!

GEORGE: Where are my sunglasses?
DAD: **I'm not sure. Where are my dadglasses?**

Why did the boy put a toad in his sister's bed? **Because he couldn't find a spider!**

What did Frankenstein say to his grandson when he noticed he'd gotten taller? **"You gruesome boy!"**

What do cannibals eat for dessert? **Chocolate-covered aunts!**

"**Mother!**" wailed Mrs. Kranky. "**You've** just drunk fifty doses of GEORGE'S MARVELOUS MEDICINE Number Four and look what one tiny spoonful did to that **little old brown hen!**" But Grandma **didn't** even hear her. Great **clouds** of **steam** were already **pouring** out of her mouth and she was **beginning** to **whistle**.

Why was the mother firefly unhappy?
Her children weren't that bright!

GIRL: Dad, I want a cat for Christmas!
DAD: **You've got to be kitten me!**

PEACHY **PUNS**
from **Around the** WORLD!

These are James's **favorites** . . .

Did you hear about the exhausted kangaroo?
She was out of bounds!

What's the difference between an American student and a UK student?
About 3,000 miles!

What did one flag say to the other?
Nothing, it just waved.

What happens when you throw a green stone in the Red Sea?
It gets wet!

What do Scotsmen eat?
Tart 'n' pie!

What is the most slippery country in the world?
Greece!

Why is Russia a very fast-moving country?
Because the people are always Russian!

What travels around the world and stays in the corner?
A stamp!

How does the sea say hello?
It waves!

How do we know that the Earth won't come to an end?
Because it's round!

Why is Dublin getting bigger?
Because it's always Dublin!

What sort of hat does a penguin wear?
An ice cap!

What pie can fly?
A magpie!

Did you hear about the wooden car with wooden wheels and a wooden engine?
It wooden go anywhere!

Which country do pirates try to sail toward?
Arrrrrrgentina!

If Ireland sank into the sea, which county would stay afloat?
Cork!

What did the tourist say about his trip to Cardiff?
He had a Wales of a time!

What do you call a chicken at the North Pole?
Lost!

What do people complain about when they visit Cuba?
Nothing—they're usually Havana great time!

What do you get when you cross a plane and a snake?
A Boeing constrictor!

James decided that he rather liked the CENTIPEDE. He was obviously a rascal, but what a change it was to hear somebody LAUGHING once in a while.

Where did the pencil go on vacation?
Pencil-vania!

What do you get when you cross a pilot with a wizard?
A flying sorcerer!

What should you write before going on vacation to the Czech Republic?
A Czech-list!

The Pelly's FISHY FUNNIES

These jokes **stink!**

Why do fish live in salt water?
Because pepper makes them sneeze!

Where do killer whales go to hear music?
The orca-stra!

What do you call a fish without an eye?
A fsh!

How do you make a goldfish old?
Take away the "g"!

"Now what on **earth** would that be?" asked the Pelican. "I have heard of a **fish-pie** and a **fish-cake** and a **fish-finger**, but I have never heard of a **fish-monger.** Are these mongers good to EAT?"

Where do fish keep their money?
In a riverbank!

What do whales eat?
Fish and ships!

Which part of a fish weighs the most?
The scales!

Which day do fish hate?
Fryday!

29

What do you get from a bad-tempered shark?
You get as far away as possible!

What's the difference between a fish and a piano?
You can't tuna fish!

Which fish only swims at night?
A starfish.

What did the sardine call the submarine?
A can of people.

What do fish take to stay healthy?
Vitamin sea!

Why was the mouse afraid of the water?
Because of the catfish!

The **BFG's** GIANT JOKES

Giant jokes for **giant** giggles!

How many balls of string would it take to reach the moon?
Just one, if it's long enough!

What is as big as a giant but weighs nothing?
Its shadow!

Where do you find giant snails?
On the end of giants' fingers!

What holds the sun up in the sky?
Sunbeams!

How do you talk to a giant?
Use big words!

Knock knock.
Who's there?
Sarah.
Sarah who?
Sarah giant living here?

What do you call a fear of giants?
Fee-fi-phobia!

Why is there always a conversation going on in the garden?
Because Jack and the beans talk.

How do you greet a three-headed giant?
Politely!

The **Giant** let out a bellow of LAUGHTER. "Just because I is a **giant**, you think I is a MAN-GOBBLING cannybull!" he shouted.

What do you call a giant's raincoat? **A tent!**

What do you call a giant's shoes? **Boats!**

What did the giant say to the lion? **"Here, kitty kitty!"**

What is even higher than a giant? **A giant's hat!**

What bugs bother giants?
Gi-ants!

What do giants call little girls?
Dinner!

What do giants call little boys?
Dessert!

What's a giant's favorite type of bean?
A human bean!

Who is the BFG's biggest enemy?
It's hard to say— they're all giant!

FUNNY BUGS

Laughs with **bite!**

What did the slug say as he slipped down the window very fast?
"How slime flies!"

What reads and lives underground?
A bookworm!

What do you do when two snails have a fight?
Leave them to slug it out!

What is the strongest animal in the world?
A snail, because it carries its house on its back!

What did the dog say to the flea?
"Stop bugging me!"

What did the snail say when he got on the turtle's shell?
"Wheeeeeeeeeeeeeeeeeeeeeeeeeeee!"

How do fleas get around?
They itch-hike!

Why was the Centipede late for the football match?
It took ages to put on its cleats!

What do you call two spiders who just got married?
Newlywebs!

What do you call little bugs who live on the moon?
Lunar-ticks!

What bugs sing a lot?
Humbugs!

What do you call a fly without wings?
A walk!

Where would you put an injured insect?
Into an ant-bulance!

"Stop **PULLING** the Earthworm's leg," the Ladybug said. This sent the Centipede into **hysterics**. "Pulling his **leg!**" he cried, **wriggling** with glee and **pointing** at the Earthworm. "Which leg am I **PULLING?** You tell me that!"

What's the brightest insect? **A firefly!**

Why did the fly fly? **Because the spider spied 'er!**

What kind of bug does a cowboy ride? **A horsefly!**

39

What do you do with a bee who's hurt his wing?
Take him to a wasp-ital!

What are caterpillars scared of?
Dog-erpillars!

Who won the fight between two silkworms?
It was a tie!

What's the difference between an elephant and a flea?
An elephant can have fleas, but a flea can't have elephants!

Why couldn't the butterfly go to the dance?
Because it was a moth-ball!

What do you call a snail on a ship?
A snailor!

How does a firefly race start?
Ready, set, glow!

What did one frog say to the other?
"Time's fun when you're having flies!"

Who is a bee's favorite composer?
Bee-thoven!

The ENORMOUS CROCO-SMILE!

Get your **teeth** into these!

What would the Enormous Crocodile be called if he was a detective?
An investi-gator!

What do you call a thieving alligator?
A crook-odile!

What has four legs, a trunk, and sunglasses?
The Enormous Crocodile on vacation!

Why don't crocodiles like fast food?
Because they can't catch it!

What's worse than a crocodile coming to dinner?
Two crocodiles coming to dinner!

The **Enormous** Crocodile laughed **SO** much his **teeth** RATTLED together like pennies in a **piggy bank**. "Crocodiles don't eat BERRIES," he said. "**We eat** little boys and girls."

What do crocodiles call children? **Appetizers!**

What do you call a crocodile who likes to go bowling? **An alley-gator!**

What's worse than two crocodiles coming to dinner? **Three crocodiles coming to dinner!**

Is it true that a crocodile won't attack you if you're carrying a flashlight? **It depends how fast you're carrying it!**

Why did the alligator get angry with his friend for crying? **They were just crocodile tears!**

CUSTOMER: I'd like to order some crocodile boots, please.
ASSISTANT: **No problem. What size boots does your crocodile wear?**

If a crocodile makes shoes, what do bananas make? **Slippers!**

Trunky's
JUMBO JOKES

For **kids** of any age—it's **irr-elephant!**

How are elephants and trees alike?
They both have trunks!

What do you call an elephant in a phone booth?
Stuck!

What did the peanut say to the elephant?
Nothing, peanuts don't talk!

What time is it when an elephant sits on your bed?
Time to get a new bed!

Where does an elephant pack his luggage?
In his trunk!

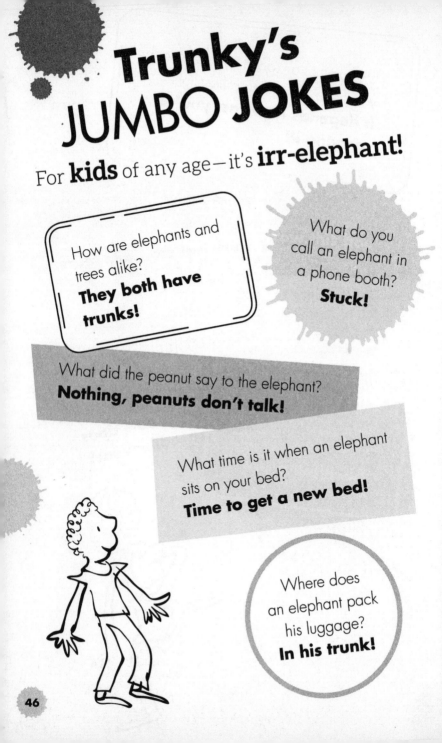

Why did the elephant leave the circus?
He was tired of working for peanuts.

What time is it when ten elephants are chasing another elephant?
Ten to one!

Then, with a crashing of branches, Trunky the Elephant came rushing out of the jungle. "That's not a bench you were going to sit on!" he bellowed. "It's the Enormous Crocodile, and he wants to EAT you all up!"

Why are elephants wrinkly?
Because they don't fit on an ironing board!

What game do elephants play when riding in the back of a car?
Squash!

What is the biggest sort of ant?
An eleph-ant!

What do you get when you cross an elephant and a fish?
Swimming trunks!

How do you know when an elephant has been in your refrigerator?
There are footprints in the butter!

What do you do with a green elephant?
Wait until it ripens!

What is big and gray and protects you from the rain?
An umbr-elephant!

What should you give an elephant who's going to be sick?
Plenty of space!

Mr. Fox's FARMYARD FUNNIES

Shhh! Don't let Boggis, Bunce, and Bean hear you **giggling!**

Where do sheep go on holiday?
The Baaaa-hamas!

What do you call a cow that eats your grass?
A lawn moo-er!

What has four legs and goes "Oom, oom"?
A cow walking backward!

Why do cows go to the theater?
To see the moo-sicals!

What do you call a pig who knows karate?
A porkchop!

"To Mr. Fox!" they all shouted, standing up and raising their GLASSES. "To Mr. Fox! Long may he live!"

Why did the lamb cross the road?
To get to the baaaa-rber shop!

What do you call a pig that's been arrested for dangerous driving?
A road hog!

What do you call a cow in a tornado?
A milkshake!

What do you call a sleeping bull?
A bulldozer!

What do you call a cow that twitches?
Beef jerky!

What is the difference between a car and a bull?
A car only has one horn!

What did one cow say to the other?
"Mooooooove over!"

What was the first animal in space?
The cow that jumped over the moon!

What is the easiest way to count a herd of cattle?
With a cow-culator!

What did the farmer call the cow that wouldn't give him any milk? **An udder failure!**

Why did the policeman give the sheep a parking ticket? **He was a baaaad driver.**

Why did the policeman give the sheep another ticket? **He made an illegal ewe turn!**

What is a cow's favorite place? **The mooseum!**

What has four wheels, gives milk, and eats grass? **A cow on a skateboard!**

What does a calf become after it's one year old?
Two years old.

COW: Moooove over!
SHEEP: **Naaaa!**

What do you give a pig with a rash?
Oinkment!

Where do cows go on Saturday night?
To the moooovies!

Why did the pig go "moo"?
Because it was learning a second language!

What do you get when you cross a dinosaur and a pig?
Jurassic pork!

What do you get from a pampered cow?
Spoiled milk!

How many sheep do you need to make a sweater?
None — sheep can't knit!

Where do horses live?
In the neigh-borhood!

What do you call a pig with no legs?
A groundhog!

What is a horse's favorite sport?
Stable tennis!

Muggle-Wump's
MONKEY
BUSINESS

Monkey around telling your friends these **jokes!**

What do you call an exploding monkey?
A baboom!

What did the banana do when the monkey chased it?
The banana split!

What did the angry monkey do?
He went bananas!

What do you call a massive gorilla?
Sir!

How do monkeys get down the stairs?
They slide down the banana-ster!

What is an ape's favorite cookie?
Chocolate chimp!

Why did the monkey like the banana?
Because it had appeal!

Where should a monkey go when she loses her tail?
To a re-tailer!

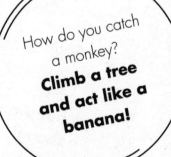

How do you catch a monkey?
Climb a tree and act like a banana!

What kind of key opens a banana?
A monkey!

How do you make a gorilla stew?
Keep it waiting for two hours!

Where do chimps get their gossip from?
The ape-vine!

"Ah-ha!" cried Muggle-Wump. "Now for the fun! Now for the greatest UPSIDE-DOWN trick of all time! Are you ready?"

What do you call a flying monkey?
A hot-air baboon!

What do you call a monkey selling potato chips?
A chip-munk!

What do monkeys do for a laugh?
Tell each other jokes about children!

Where do monkeys sleep at summer camp?
In their ape-ricots!

What do you call a baby ape?
A chimp off the old block!

What do apes use to fix their houses?
Monkey wrenches!

Why shouldn't you get into a fight with an ape?
They use gorilla warfare!

When do monkeys fall from the sky?
During Ape-ril showers!

What do chimps wear when they're cooking?
Ape-rons!

Why do apes tell such bad stories?
Because they have no tails!

Why are apes so noisy?
They were raised in a zoo!

Why did the monkey put a net over his head?
He wanted to catch his breath!

Why did the giant ape climb up the skyscraper?
The elevator was broken!

Why do gorillas have big nostrils?
Because they have big fingers!

What do you call a gorilla in a tree?
Branch manager!

Dirty Beasts and ANIMAL ANTICS

Funnier than a **trip** to the **zoo!**

What did the snake say when he was offered a piece of cheese?
"Thank you, I'll just have a slither."

Why do animals wear fur coats?
Because they would look silly in plastic raincoats!

What do you do if your dog chews up a dictionary?
Take the words out of his mouth!

What do you call a girl with a frog on her head?
Lily!

What goes tick-tock, bow-wow, tick-tock, bow-wow?
A watch dog!

Where do mice moor their boats?
At the hickory dickory dock.

What is a cat's favorite movie?
The Sound of Meow-sic!

How does a dog stop a video?
He presses the paws button!

What is it called when you lend money to a bison?
A buff-a-loan!

On which side do tigers have the most stripes?
The outside!

"She is the Giraffe!" the Pelican answered. "Is she not wonderful? Her LEGS are on the ground floor and her head is looking out of the top WINDOW!"

What is a cheetah's favorite meal?
Fast food!

What happened to the frog's car?
It got toad away!

Why was the cat afraid of the tree?
Because of the bark!

What does a cat say when somebody steps on its tail?
"Me-ow!"

What do you get when you plant a frog? **A cr-oak tree!**

How do you stop a dog barking in the back seat of a car? **Put him in the front seat!**

What is the quietest kind of dog? **A hush puppy!**

How is a dog like a telephone? **It has collar ID!**

Why do cows wear bells? **Because their horns don't work!**

What did the carrot say to the rabbit? **"Do you want to grab a bite?"**

What kind of cat should you never play games with?
A cheetah!

What is black and white and red all over?
A panda with a rash!

Why are giraffes so slow to apologize?
It takes them a long time to swallow their pride!

What do you call a dog that likes bubble baths?
A sham-poodle!

How did Noah see the animals in the ark at night?
With flood lights!

What happened when the lion ate the comedian?
He felt funny!

What's black and white and red all over?
A blushing zebra!

What did the mother buffalo say to her son before he went to school?
"Bison!"

What kind of dog always runs a fever?
A hot dog!

What do you do if your cat swallows your pencil?
Use a pen!

Which pine has the longest needles?
A porcupine!

What kind of cars do cats drive?
Cat-illacs!

What do you call a deer with no eyes?
No eye-deer!

There were ten cats in a boat and one jumped out. How many were left?
None—they were all copycats!

What's black and white and red all over?
A sunburnt zebra!

What is a young dog's favorite kind of pizza?
Pupperoni!

How does a mouse feel after it takes a shower?
Squeaky clean!

What do camels use to hide themselves?
Camel-flage!

What do you get if you cross an owl with a lion?
A growl!

What do you call a messy hippo?
A hippopota-mess!

What is a frog's favorite year?
A leap year!

Where do felines buy their clothes from?
Cat-alogs!

Where do canines buy their clothes from?
Dog-ologs!

Why did the pony go to the doctor?
He was feeling a little hoarse!

What do you call
a pile of kittens?
A meow-ntain!

Why are frogs so
happy?
**Because they eat
what bugs them!**

What kinds of books do rabbits like to read?
Books with hoppy endings!

When a duck has no money,
what does he say to the waiter?
"Just put it on my bill!"

Where do
penguins go to
dance?
**The snow
ball!**

Squirrel NUTS

Nuttier than **Wonka's** Nutty Crunch Surprise!

What do you get if you cross a suitcase and a squirrel?
A nut-case!

Where did the squirrel store his food?
In his pan-tree!

How do you catch a squirrel?
Climb up a tree and act like a nut!

How do you catch a sophisticated squirrel?
Climb up a tree and act like a cashew nut!

What do squirrels eat on vacation?
Coconuts!

Why did the red squirrel ask for help with some work?
It was a bit of a gray area!

"All right," said Mr. Wonka, "**stop** here for a **moment** and **catch** your **BREATH,** and take a **peek** through the glass panel of this **door.** But **don't** go in! Whatever you do, **don't** go into THE **NUT ROOM!** If you go in, you'll **disturb** the **SQUIRRELS!**"

Why couldn't the squirrel eat the walnut?
It was one tough nut to crack!

Why do woodland animals not eat all their food in one go?
They like to squirrel it away!

Why did the squirrel take apart the car?
To get down to the nuts and bolts!

Why can't you be friends with a squirrel?
They drive everyone nuts!

JOKES for TWITS!

WARNING: These jokes **stink!**

How do you keep a skunk from smelling? **Hold its nose!**

How many skunks does it take to make a big stink? **A phew!**

Why does a giraffe have such a long neck? **Because its feet reek!**

Why do skunks like old movies?
Because they are black and white.

What I am trying to tell you is that **Mr. Twit** was a foul and SMELLY old man.

My dog has no nose. How does he smell? **Awful!**

Why can't you hear a pterodactyl going to the toilet?
Because it has a silent "p"!

What did one eye say to the other?
"Between you and me, something smells."

What's black and white, black and white, black and white and green?
Three skunks fighting over a pickle!

What did one snowman say to the other?
"Do you smell carrots?"

What sorts of books do skunks like to read?
Best-smellers!

Why is your nose in the middle of your face?
Because it's the scent-er.

What always smells best at the dinner table?
Your nose!

What did one toilet say to the other?
"You look flushed!"

What color socks do bears wear? **They don't wear socks—they go around with bear feet!**

Did you hear the joke about the gym sock? **You wouldn't want to—it absolutely stinks!**

If athletes get athlete's foot, what do fighter pilots get? **Missile-toe!**

What does a pirate call the pattern on his smelly socks? **Arrrrrrrr-gyle!**

Why did the pig take a bath? **The farmer said "hogwash"!**

Why shouldn't you tease eggs about their smell? **They can't take a yolk!**

What do you call a helicopter with a skunk for a pilot? **A smelly-copter!**

What has a bottom at the top? **Your legs!**

What's the difference between cabbage and boogers? **Kids don't eat cabbage!**

What did the dog say after his third bath? **"Why do I still smell like a wet dog?"**

What do you get if you cross a skunk with a boomerang?
A bad smell that keeps coming back!

Why did the man hate hearing jokes about his feet?
They were too corny!

What do you call a dinosaur with smelly feet?
Ex-stinked!

What did the smelly judge say?
"Odor in court!"

The MOST MONSTROUS Gags EVER!

Watch out!
These ones are frighteningly **funny.**

How can you tell the difference between a rabbit and a red-eyed monster?
Just try getting a red-eyed monster into a rabbit hutch.

What do you do with a green monster?
Put it in the sun until it ripens!

Why did the monster paint himself in rainbow colors?
Because he wanted to hide in the crayon box!

What do you give a monster with big feet?
Big slippers!

"Look out!" cried the BFG. "It's the BLOODBOTTLER!"

Why was the big, hairy, two-headed monster top of the class at school?
Because two heads are better than one!

What did the big, hairy monster do when he lost a hand?
He went to the second-hand shop!

How do you stop a monster digging up your garden?
Take his spade away!

What does a polite monster say when he meets you for the first time?
"Pleased to eat you!"

Why did all the food get eaten at the monster's party?
Because everyone was goblin!

What kind of monster can sit on the end of your finger?
The boogeyman!

Why did the big, hairy monster give up boxing?
Because he didn't want to spoil his looks!

What happens if a big, hairy monster sits in front of you at the cinema?
You miss most of the film!

Why did the two cyclopses fight?
They could never see eye to eye on anything!

How do you know when there's a monster under your bed?
Your nose touches the ceiling!

What is the best way to speak to a monster?
From a long distance!

Why did the monster have green ears and a red nose?
So that he could hide in rhubarb patches!

How do you tell a good monster from a bad one?
If it's a good one you will be able to talk about it later!

What's big, heavy, furry, dangerous and has sixteen wheels?
A monster on roller skates!

What do you call a huge, ugly, slobbering, furry monster with cotton balls in his ears? **Anything you like—he can't hear you!**

Why couldn't the swamp monster go to the party? **Because he was bogged down in his work!**

Who won the witch beauty contest? **No one!**

How do you know that there's a monster in your bath? **You can't get the shower curtain closed!**

How do you get six monsters in a cookie jar? **Take the cookies out first!**

Why was the monster standing on his head? **He was turning things over in his mind!**

What should you do if a monster runs through your front door? **Run through the back door!**

What do little vampires learn at school?
The alpha-bat!

What sort of monster loves to party?
The boogie-man!

Why are monsters so forgetful?
Everything goes in one ear and out the five others!

What did the monster say about his eight arms?
They come in very handy!

What do monsters like on their sandwiches?
Ghoul-slaw!

WHICH One's WITCH?

These jokes are the Grand High Witch's worst **nightmare!**

How did the witch look after she was run over by a car?
Tire-d!

What is evil, ugly and goes round and round?
A witch in a revolving door!

What is green on the outside and evil and ugly on the inside?
A witch dressed as a cucumber!

What happens if you see twin witches?
You won't be able to tell which witch is which!

What does a witch get if she is a poor traveler?
Broom sick!

Why did the witch put her broom in the wash?
She wanted a clean sweep!

Why did the stupid witch keep her clothes in the fridge?
She liked to have something cool to slip into in the evenings!

Why did the witch give up fortune telling?
There was no future in it!

What has six legs and flies?
A witch giving her cat a ride!

What has handles and flies?
A witch in a trash can!

What is evil, ugly, and bounces?
A witch on a trampoline!

What did the doctor say to the witch in hospital?
With any luck you'll soon be well enough to get up for a spell!

How do witches
lose weight?
**They join Weight
Witches!**

What
do witches
race on?
Vroom-sticks!

Have you heard about the
good weather witch?
**She's forecasting
sunny spells!**

How is the witch's football
team doing?
**They're going through a
successful spell!**

What makes
more noise than
an angry witch?
**Two angry
witches!**

What happened to the witch with
an upside-down nose?
**Every time she sneezed,
her hat blew off!**

What happened when the witch went for a job as a TV presenter?
The producer said that she had the perfect face for radio!

Why did the witch join the soccer team?
Because she heard they were looking for a new sweeper!

Who turns the lights off at Halloween?
The lights witch!

What do you call a witch with one leg?
Eileen!

What is the best way of stopping infection from witch bites?
Don't bite any witches!

A real WITCH gets the same pleasure from SQUELCHING a child as you get from eating a plateful of strawberries and thick cream.

What do witches sing at Christmas?
"Deck the Halls with Poison Ivy!"

What is old, ugly, and bright blue?
A witch holding her breath!

What happens to naughty witches at school?
They get ex-spelled!

What do you call a witch who likes the beach but is afraid of the water?
A chicken sand-witch!

Why do witches like cooking with toads' legs?
A child's legs wouldn't fit in the cauldron!

What do you get if you cross a witch and an iceberg?
A cold spell!

What do you call a nice, friendly witch?
A failure!

What goes cackle, cackle, cackle . . . BOOM?
A witch in a minefield!

What is a witch with allergies called?
An itchy witchy!

What's the best way of talking to a witch?
Over the phone!

What do you call it when a witch's cat falls off her broomstick?
A cat-astrophe!

Why didn't the witch sing at the concert?
She had a frog in her throat!

What has six legs and flies?
Three witches on one broomstick!

Formula 86
FUNNIES

Make your friends **squeak** with **laughter!**

What do cats call
mice on skateboards?
Meals on wheels!

When is it unlucky to
see a black cat cross
your path?
**When you're a
mouse!**

What do
angry mice send
each other at
Christmas?
**Cross-mouse
cards!**

What did the cat
have for breakfast?
Mice Krispies!

What goes
dot-dot-dash-squeak?
Mouse code!

What is a mouse's favorite game?
Hide and squeak!

Who are small, furry, and good with swords?
The Three Mouse-keteers!

How do you save a drowning mouse?
Mouse-to-mouse resuscitation!

When is it time to oil your mouse?
When it starts squeaking!

What do you get when you lock mice in the freezer?
Mice cubes!

What do mice like for dessert?
Mice cream!

When do mice need to carry an umbrella?
When it's raining cats and dogs!

Why is there no such thing as a mousefish?
Because of all the catfish!

Which Roman emperor was actually a mouse?
Julius Cheese-r.

What do mice do when they're at home?
Mouse-work!

Bruno looked down at his paws. He jumped. "Good grief!" he cried. "I am a MOUSE! You wait till my father hears about this!" "He may think it's an improvement," I said.

What is hairy and lives on a man's face?
A mouse-tache!

How do mice celebrate when they move?
They throw a mouse-warming party!

Wonka
WISECRACKS

Sweeten up even the most **boring** adults!

What do Oompa-Loompas use to clean their teeth?
Candy floss!

Did you hear the joke about the chocolate sauce?
I'm not telling you. You might spread it!

What's the best thing to put into a chocolate bar?
Your teeth!

What is better than seeing a chocolate river?
Drinking a chocolate river!

What did the bubblegum say to the shoe? **"I'm stuck on you!"**

Why was the cookie sad? **She was feeling crumby!**

What do Oompa-Loompas make sandwiches with? **Shortbread!**

What kind of bear has no teeth? **A gummy bear!**

"My **dear** boy," said Grandpa Joe, raising himself up a little HIGHER on his pillow, "Mr. Willy Wonka is the most amazing, the most **fantastic**, the most extraordinary chocolate maker the world has **ever** seen! I thought **everybody** knew that!"

What do you call a lamb covered in chocolate?
A chocolate baaaa!

What sort of keys do kids like to carry around with them?
Coo-keys!

Why did the ice cream truck get stuck?
Because of the rocky road!

Why did the jelly doughnut go to the dentist?
Because it lost its filling!

What happened to the chocolate factory?
It melted!

What kind of sweet is never on time?
Choco-late!

Where do you go to learn how to make ice cream?
Sundae school!

How do you make milk shake?
Give it a fright!

Knock knock!
Who's there?
Banana!
Banana who?
Banana split so ice creamed!

What cake is so hard it breaks your teeth?
Marble pound cake!

How do you make an apple turnover?
Push it down a hill!

What did the doughnut wear to bed?
Jammies!

Why do you put candles on the top of a birthday cake?
It would be too difficult to put them on the bottom!

What did the newspaper say to the ice cream?
"What's the scoop?"

What do you give a sick lemon?
Lemon-aid!

How do astronauts eat their ice cream?
In floats!

Why did the giant put clouds in his pancakes?
To make them light and fluffy!

MORE JOKES for TWITS!

WARNING: These jokes get **hairy!**

What do you call a goat with a beard?
Goatee!

What did the man say to his barber?
"I moustache you a question, but I'll shave it for later."

Who shaves ten times a day and still has a beard?
The barber!

What happens when bearded men sunbathe?
They get sideburns!

Mr. Twit felt that his hairiness made him look terrifically wise and grand. But in truth he was neither of these things. Mr. Twit was a twit. He was born a twit. And now at the age of sixty, he was a BIGGER twit than ever.

What did the man say about his enormous beard?
"It just grew on me!"

How do barbers make phone calls?
They cut them short!

Why did Mr. Twit put a rabbit on his head?
He wanted a full head of hare!

Why are people always asking Mr. Twit to turn round?
They can't tell which side of him is which!

What do you call a pen with no hair?
A bald point pen!

Who never gets their hair wet in the shower?
A bald man!

Why did the bald man go outside?
To get some fresh hair!

Why doesn't Mr. Twit want to shave his beard?
He's attached to it!

What kind of beard does the sea have?
Wavy!

What's the difference between Mr. Twit's beard and a fridge?
The food in a fridge is fresh!

Why do barbers make good drivers?
Because they know all the short cuts!

Matilda MAGIC!

Funnies to make your friends cry…with **laughter!**

Did you hear about the magic tractor? **It turned into a field!**

In what way is Miss Trunchbull mean but fair? **She's mean to EVERYONE!**

What do you call a ghost whisperer who has escaped from prison? **A medium at large!**

Why did Miss Trunchbull give her whole class a zero on their tests? **She couldn't give them anything lower!**

"Do YOU think that all children's books ought to have FUNNY bits in them?" Miss Honey asked.

"I do," Matilda said. "Children are NOT so serious as grown-ups and they LOVE to LAUGH."

Why is your newt called Tiny?
Because he's my-newt!

Why did the clock get sent to see the Trunchbull?
For tocking too much!

TRUNCHBULL: Why aren't you standing at the end of the line like I told you?
PUPIL: **I tried, but there was somebody standing there already!**

What's the difference between a hungry man and Bruce Bogtrotter? **One longs to eat and the other eats too long!**

What did the gopher say to the librarian? **"Please may I burrow this book?"**

Why was Mr. Wormwood angry when Matilda put glue in his hat? **It was a hat trick!**

MISS HONEY: You missed school yesterday, didn't you? LAVENDER: **No, I didn't miss it in the slightest!**

What is Miss Honey's favorite nation? **Expla-nation!**

Why was the math book always unhappy? **Because it had lots of problems!**

DAD: What did you learn at school today? SON: **Not enough— they said I have to go back again tomorrow!**

Why did the music teacher need a ladder? **To reach the high notes!**

What kind of schoolbag is always tired? **A knapsack!**

Why did Bruce Bogtrotter eat his homework? **The teacher told him it was a piece of cake!**

And finally...

THE **Whizzpoppers!**

According to the BFG,
whizzpopping is a sign of
happiness!

What's the difference between
a symphony and a whizzpop?
**One is music to your ear
and the other is music
from your rear!**

What do you get if you
cross onions and beans?
Tear gas!

What's
invisible and smells
like carrots?
**A bunny
whizzpop!**

Why is a whizzpop the sharpest thing in the world?
It can go through almost any fabric and it never leaves a hole!

"**Kings** and Queens are **WHIZZPOPPING**. Presidents are **WHIZZPOPPING**. Glamorous film stars are **WHIZZPOPPING**. Little **babies** are **WHIZZPOPPING**. But where **I** come from, it is **not** polite to talk about it."

What are the queen's whizzpops made of?
Noble gas!

Somewhere in the world a person whizzpops every other second.
We must find this person and stop them!

Did you hear about the man who was giving out anti-whizzpop leaflets?
He accidentally let one rip!

Why couldn't the skeleton whizzpop?
It didn't have the guts to do it!

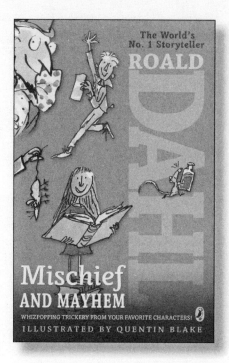

Professional tricksters put your cunning to the test. Inside this wicked little book, you'll find step-by-step instructions for making mischief and mayhem as well as outrageous jokes, fiendish quizzes, and a few smelly surprises. Includes extracts from *Charlie and the Chocolate Factory*, *Matilda*, *The BFG*, *The Witches*, and more. Like *The Missing Golden Ticket and Other Splendiferous Secrets*, this book is a wonderful complement to Roald Dahl novels, with tons of great extras fans will love. It's the perfect way to complete your Dahl collection!

A brilliant extension to Dahl's wonderful stories, this book gives fascinating insights into the characters and events from Roald Dahl's writing in a humorous, exciting and downright gloriumptious way. For the very first time, the stories behind the stories are brought to life in this interactive book. Inside, Quentin Blake's iconic illustrations are combined with imagined letters, artifacts and news clippings, and editing notes from Dahl himself, to bring all of Roald Dahl's characters alive.

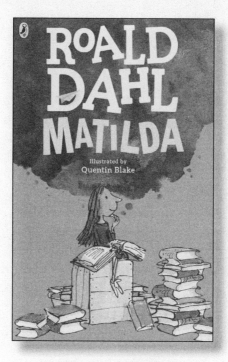

"The Trunchbull"
is no match for Matilda!

Matilda is a sweet, exceptional young girl, but her parents
think she's just a nuisance. She expects school to be differ-
ent, but there she has to face Miss Trunchbull, a kid-hating
terror of a headmistress. When Matilda is attacked by the
Trunchbull, she suddenly discovers she has a remarkable
power with which to fight back. It'll take a superhuman
genius to give Miss Trunchbull what she deserves, and
Matilda may be just the one to do it!

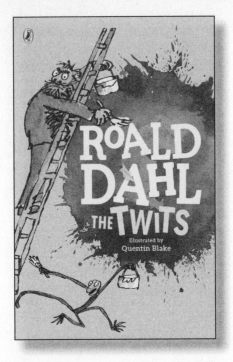

How do you outwit a Twit?

Mr. and Mrs. Twit are the smelliest, nastiest, ugliest people in the world. They hate everything—except playing mean jokes on each other, catching innocent birds to put in their Bird Pies, and making their caged monkeys, the Muggle-Wumps, stand on their heads all day. But the Muggle-Wumps have had enough. They don't just want out, they want revenge.

Captured by a giant!

The BFG is no ordinary bone-crunching giant. He is far too nice and jumbly. It's lucky for Sophie that he is. Had she been carried off in the middle of the night by the Bloodbottler, or any of the other giants—rather than the BFG—she would have soon become breakfast. When Sophie hears that the giants are flush-bunking off to England to swollomp a few nice little chiddlers, she decides she must stop them once and for all. And the BFG is going to help her!

Willy Wonka's famous chocolate factory is opening at last!

But only five lucky children will be allowed inside. And the winners are: Augustus Gloop, an enormously fat boy whose hobby is eating; Veruca Salt, a spoiled-rotten brat whose parents are wrapped around her little finger; Violet Beauregarde, a dim-witted gum-chewer with the fastest jaws around; Mike Teavee, a toy pistol–toting gangster-in-training who is obsessed with television; and Charlie Bucket, Our Hero, a boy who is honest and kind, brave and true, and good and ready for the wildest time of his life!

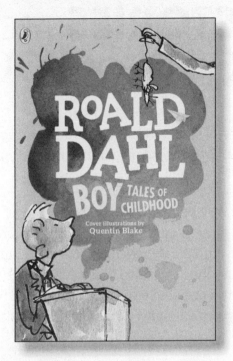

Where did Roald Dahl get all of his wonderful ideas for stories?

From his own life, of course! As full of excitement and the unexpected as his world-famous, bestselling books, Roald Dahl's tales of his own childhood are completely fascinating and fiendishly funny. Did you know that Roald Dahl nearly lost his nose in a car accident? Or that he was once a chocolate candy tester for Cadbury's? Have you heard about his involvement in the Great Mouse Plot of 1924? If not, you don't yet know all there is to know about Roald Dahl. Sure to captivate and delight you, the boyhood antics of this master storyteller are not to be missed!

STORIES ARE GOOD FOR YOU.

Roald Dahl said,
"If you have good thoughts, they will shine out of your face like sunbeams and you will always look lovely."

We believe in doing good things.
That's why 10 percent of all Roald Dahl income* goes to our charity partners. We have supported causes including: specialist children's nurses, grants for families in need, and educational outreach programs. Thank you for helping us to sustain this vital work.

Find out more at roalddahl.com

The Roald Dahl Charitable Trust is a registered UK charity (no. 1119330).
* All author payments and royalty income net of third-party commissions.